I'm Not Getting
(I'm Getting Better at Denial)

101 Humorous Tips for Feeling Good About Being a Midlife Woman

by Leigh Anne Jasheway

Illustrated by Deborah Kaye

Comedy Workout Publishing

Eugene, OR

Look for these other books by Leigh Anne Jasheway:

Bedtime Stories for Dogs
Bedtime Stories for Cats
The Rules for Dogs
The Rules for Cats
Don't Get Mad, Get Funny: A Light-hearted Approach to Stress Management
Give Me a Break: For Women Who Have Too Much to Do
Driving for Idiots

Acknowledgments

This book contains little, if any, factual information, except, the part on duct tape and Kegel exercises. And something else, but I can't remember what it was.   I'd like to thank my dogs, their acupuncturist, my massage therapist, my personal assistant who always yells at me "That's too personal!," my friend Jan who often claims she doesn't know me, and my friend Rhonda who thinks my jokes are funny even if I just woke her up. Not to mention my spouse who doesn't get it most of the time and my mom who'd prefer to remain anonymous.

Introduction

We're strong women. Empowered women. Some of us are brazen even. Why is it then that most of us over-forty females have at least nine different "anti-aging" products in our medicine chest? If we're going to spend money on stuff that doesn't work, why not "anti-dirty laundry," "anti-unbalanced checkbook," "anti-having to work with moron," and "anti-falling in the toilet in the middle of the night and getting a butt hickey" products? Why isn't someone out there working on those? Hmmm?

Yeah, we're strong. Empowered. Brazen. And completely, totally in denial. Don't deny it. You know it's true. In fact, you almost didn't buy this book because it had the word "mid-life" in the title, now did you?

Yep, no matter how enlightened we are, the words "middle aged" still depress us. "Middle?" We don't want to be in the middle (well, there is that one fantasy, but that's another story...). We want to be on top! Not to mention that the word "middle" reminds us of our own "middle," which no matter how hard we try, seems to grow a little every year. As I recently told a friend, "The girth does not belong to us, we belong to the girth."

Then there's the "Age" part of "middle age." We don't mind the word when someone says, *"You don't look your age."* But we know that sooner or time will catch up with us and we'll start hearing things like, *"You're really light on your feet for someone your age."* Or we'll start saying things like *"When I was your age, nice girls pierced their ears, not their nipples."*

So we deny our age. Politely. Angrily. Through a layer of anti-aging products. While working out. While eating fettucini Alfredo. While wearing that miniskirt from the 70s as a turban around our thinning hair. While dismembering Barbie.

You know you're in middle-age denial if:

- You think you still look twenty-something. From the back. At night. In the fog.
- You sprinkle bran flakes on your Captain Crunch cereal every morning.
- You smear Vaseline on your mirror, for that softer, out-of-focus look.

- You hear two voices in your head. The Goddess voice, which says "Big thighs and a rounder belly are beautiful. One day they will be worshipped!" And the Barbie voice, which says "Until that day comes, if you do 350 butt crunches every 15 minutes, you will look like Jane Fonda. Or, at least, her less famous second cousin Wanda Fonda."

So, go ahead, accept your denial. Embrace it. Celebrate it even. Only then can you feel better about it.

Now, take a deep breath. And join us in these tongue-in-cheek tips for aging gracefully and denying you're doing it at all.

1.   Next time you're feeling depressed about your body, take a
      long look in the mirror. Are your breasts still higher than
      your waist? Is there no duct tape involved? Then you are
      still one hot and sexy woman!

2.   Sometimes fashion trends are worth paying attention to. Like those really big jeans all the kids wearing these days. Not only are they comfortable, but you can carry everything you need in your pockets -- your keys, your wallet, your minivan...

3. The words "for someone your age" don't need to scare you. For example: "You certainly have nice legs for someone your age" isn't too bad. "You certainly are orgasmic for someone your age" is even better.

4.   There are so many products on the market to camouflage the signs of aging such as wrinkles, gray hair, and love handles. Just be careful: if you camouflage yourself too well people may not see you at all. Instead of trying to blend into the scenery, stand out and be noticed! Wear a bright orange vest and a purple g-string. Just don't hang out with drunk guys with rifles.

5. If the doctor tells you you're losing estrogen, don't sit there and do nothing. Be proactive. Put a picture of your estrogen on flyers and post them all around town. Offer a large reward. If you're lucky, maybe some good Samaritan will return your estrogen to you, no harm done.

6.   So what if your breasts have lost some elasticity. It's not like you were going to shoot them across the room. Were you?

7.   As we get older, many women tend to develop "overactive bladder syndrome." This can be a good thing because it means that part of your body is still active. And it's sure a lot easier than trying to get your spleen to work out.

8.   On those long, gray days, do you sometimes depressed and kind of blue? You've probably got S.A.D. – Shitty Attitude Disorder. Here's what you should do: slap your therapist; it'll make you feel so much better.

9.   Love handles make it a lot easier to keep a hula hoop going.

10.   Today is a good day to commit to doing something you've
      wanted to do since you were a kid: take tap-dancing lessons,
      learn to fly, become a ballerina astronaut superhero
      President. After all, isn't it about time this country had a
      ballerina astronaut superhero President? And aren't you
      just the woman for the job?

11.   Face it: if there really was a fountain of youth, there'd probably be pigeons bathing in it, and you'd feel compelled to clean up after them!

12.   If you decide on plastic surgery, find a really good doctor. There's nothing worse for your self esteem than showing off your new face only to have someone point out the recycling code stamped on your forehead!

13.   You can look at the glass half empty. You can look at the glass half full. Or you can look at the glass and wonder, "Did I or didn't I just drink my soy milk?"

14.   Sometimes the best way to feel more in control of your life is to take control. Did you know that when in a car with a man, the majority of women let him drive? Why is that? Why do we automatically gravitate to the passenger's seat like there's a vibrator built in? Go ahead, call dibs on the steering wheel!

15.   Although they can sound enticing, free in-store beauty
       make-overs can be a blow to your self esteem. Who needs
       white-coated women with over-plucked eyebrows announcing
       over the store intercom that your pores need to be cleaned
       with an industrial wet-dry vac? Just call your mother. At
       least when she humiliates you it's one-on-one.

16.   Kegel exercises are really important as we get older. It doesn't matter if the rest of you is soft and flabby, as long as you have vaginal walls of steel.

17.   How many times have you tried to lose weight? Why not try losing depth instead? If you can't be thin, at least you can be shallow.

18.   We can learn a little something from midlife men, can't we? For example, if your breasts are starting to sag, why not grow out your armpit hair and do the old comb-over?

19.   So what if you've got laugh lines and worry lines? Imagine if you had lines on your face for every other emotion you ever experienced… how about envy lines, embarrassment lines, confusion lines, orgasm lines…? Well, maybe orgasm lines wouldn't be so bad.

20. The only part of the mammogram that really pinches is when they try to move your breasts as far away from the rest of your body as possible. Actually, while your breasts are being x-rayed, you can wait in the lobby for them to return.

X-RAY

21. You shouldn't get your tongue pierced. When you yell, "Get down here right this instant!" to your kids, you don't want them misunderstanding you and thinking you said, "Sure, you can go to the coed sleepover!"

22. It's hard to follow your bliss when you can't really see it. Unless you put on your glasses, you could be following someone else's bliss without even knowing it! And then who knows where you'd end up?

23.   If you wake up with an uncontrollable urge to listen to Perry Como records, you could be "Peri-menopausal." No need to panic, unless you actually go out and buy a Perry Como record. Then, you might want to check with your doctor.

24.   Want to spice up your life? Buy one of those aromatherapy machines that comes with scent crystals to set different moods. Put on "Happy" or "Sexy" or "Bitchy..." whatever works for you.

25. Before getting liposuction, consider these other, cheaper procedures:

- Rap-o-suction - relocation of people playing rap music from a 100 mile radius

- Yap-o-suction - surgical extraction of people who won't shut up

- Crap-o-suction - self-explanatory

- Life-o-suction - Mandatory incarceration for people who suck the life out of you

26.   Half of women say their interest in sex doesn't decrease while they're going through menopause. 80% however, do report a decrease in their ability to tolerate morons.

27.   Did you ever try those cottage cheese diets that were so popular a while back? And now what do your thighs look like? Cottage cheese? Large curd? Seems like plenty of reason to stop dieting immediately.

28.   If you're lying about your age and someone questions how you could possibly be the mother of teenagers at your age, say they were adopted. You know that's what your kids tell their friends about you.

29.   Did you burn your bra when you were young to declare your independence? Well, these days, you probably need your bra, but here are six things you may be able to burn instead: your thong undies, your birth control pills (be absolutely sure first!), the paid mortgage on your house, your exes' golf clubs, any item of clothing that screams 'disco,' and your subscription to *Young Skinny Women Who Puke Up Their Lunch* magazine.

30. Which kind of Crone do you want to be? Cranky Retentive Old Near-sighted and Edgy? Or Creative Real Open-minded Non-conforming and Erotic?

31. If this is the year you've decided to be adventurous, why not get a tattoo? A tattoo of your address and phone number could not only be attractive, but very useful in those memory emergencies.

32.   Chinese Herbs can be very beneficial for midlife women. So can Jewish Herbs, African American Herbs, and even White Anglo-Saxon Protestant Herbs, providing they've all learned how to keep their pants up and put the toilet seat down.

33.   Cellulite is not something to stress over. Celibacy – now there's something to stress over!!

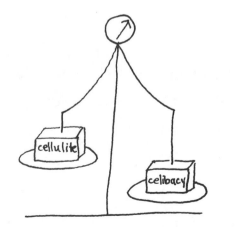

34. Don't try to do menopause alone. Join your local menopause network. Better yet, join the Hell's Angels.

35.   Life is too short to hold your stomach or your opinions in.
      Go ahead, let it all hang out.

36.   If you're thinking about getting a pet, consider a Sharpei.
      Looking into her wrinkled face every morning will make your
      skin seem smooth and firm in comparison.

Sharpei   You

37.   Have you noticed recently that you've become invisible to people? Here's a great way to get seen again: The next time you're in a department store and the sales clerk can't see you, fake an orgasm. Loud. Into the intercom. That should get everyone's attention. You will undoubtedly get served right away!

38. Don't think of it as middle-aged weight gain. Think of it as personal growth.

39. For mood swings, try yam cream. And if you feel like smearing on some marshmallows and brown sugar too, who's gonna stop you?

40. So what if you can't remember people's names any more? Don't lose sleep over it. The next time you see someone whose name escapes you, instead of racking your brain trying to think of it, simply say, "My God! You look great! Have you lost weight?" She'll be so happy, she'll never realize you have no idea who she is.

41. Feeling overwhelmed by trying to do it all? Try this quick remedy: For an entire month, stop reading any magazine that insists that you can make a gourmet meal for twenty, grout your tub, negotiate world peace, and look fifteen years younger – all on your lunch hour. Instead, read things that don't inflate your expectations, like the back of your shampoo bottle. "Lather, rinse, repeat." You can do that.

42. You know it's time for a new bra when one breast enters the room before the other. "Would you hurry up and get in here!" are not words you want to deliver to your cleavage.

43.   You can have an exciting sex life no matter what your age. The trick is to try new things, like making love in exotic locations. Try Maui or an elevator or the other side of the bed.

44.   A quick quiz: During perimenopause, your period may (a) get heavier, (b) get lighter, (c) get a perm, (d) get an apartment, (e) get a life of it's own. If you answered a, b, or e, you're one smart cookie! If your period gets its own apartment, don't offer to pay the rent.

45. If you are considering a second career, use your wisdom and experience to avoid some of the mistakes you made the first time around. Avoid, for example, any job where you have to wear a paper hat and call a teenage boy "Sir."

46.   Here's something you'll never, ever, have to do again unless
       you want to: Fake orgasm, fake cuddling, or fake interest.

47.   There are so many exercise videos on the market, it's hard
       to choose one that's just right for you. Here's a tip: forget
       Sweating to the Oldies -- it'll just make you feel old and
       sweaty. And watching Richard Simmons may even make you
       feel macho.

48.   You decide which is better for you: multiple vitamins or multiple orgasms?

49.   The best thing about marrying a younger man is that it's easier to get along with your mother-in-law if you're both the same age.

you

your mother-in-law

50. If you're planning to try hormone replacement therapy, don't let the hormones you still have find out about it. They'll just get all jealous and huffy and be really rude to the new hormones, taunting them and calling them names.

51.   Those slenderizing swimsuits are fine up to a point. But remember: for every action, there is an equal and opposite reaction.   So for every five pounds your suit may hold in, there's got to be five pounds hanging out somewhere else. If you find your hips flapping under your arms, you're asking too much from your swimsuit!

52.   You can still be a natural woman. It just takes a little more
      artifice these days.

53.   Forget Caller ID, how about Continuous Remind, a service
      that would remind you who you called and why you called
      them. Not to mention, who you are.

54.   Maybe you aren't Zena, Warrior Princess. But that doesn't
      mean you have to turn into Gina, Worrier Princess, Zena's
      less perky-chested cousin whose special powers are anxiety,
      self-doubt, and fingernails chewed down to the stubs. The
      next time you feel Gina emerging, use all your superpowers
      to keep her away. Or use a super maxipad!

55.   So what if you've grown a little moustache? As long as you haven't grown a little penis, you're fine!

56.   According to a recent survey, 72% of women are dissatisfied with their thighs and 60% are ashamed of their hips. Very few, however, were disappointed in their pancreas. Let's hear it for the pancreas!

57.   Girdles are popular again, only now they're called "Body Shapers." Just be careful to choose one that shapes your body naturally, not into something like an oak tree or the Pentagon building.

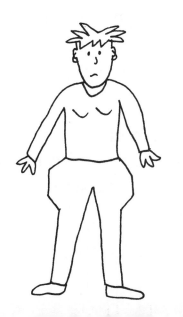

58.   Sure, it's scary when you realize you've turned into your
      mother. But not as scary as that Franz Kafka story "The
      Metamorphosis," in which he turned into a cockroach. It's
      all a matter of perspective.

59.   If you have a tummy tuck, make sure the surgeon tucks it somewhere you can find it again later when you need it. You don't want to put on an old coat five years later and discover your tummy in one of the pockets.

60.   Does it seem sometimes that the world is out to destroy our self esteem? Avoid, at all costs, any company that makes you feel worse about yourself. For example, those commuter airlines with a box at ticket check-in that says, "If your hips won't fit in here, you're too big for our ride." That's just rude!

If your hips won't fit in this box...

61.   Now is a good time to start adding new words to your every day vocabulary. Try: curvaceous, ripe, Rubenesque, pendulous, bodacious. If you don't have much extra room in your memory, you could dump a few old words, such as: firm, perky, and "Of course I will!"

62.   Next time you go to the gynecologist, wear spurs. Hey, your feet are in the stirrups, you might as well dress the part. And if anything doesn't go as planned, dig in your heels and yell, "Whoa, there!"

63.   Go ahead – tell everyone exactly what you think of them.
      Tomorrow you probably won't remember what you said or
      even who they are!

64.   Do you get depressed every time you look at a picture of
      yourself when you were younger, firmer, and, well, younger
      and firmer is enough... Here's a great pick-me-up. Caption
      all your photos. Under a photo of you in a sexy nighty:
      "Have you seen my g-spot?"

65.   Is it time for a mammogram? Don't stress out about it.
      Sure, they squeeze your breasts flat, but they'll bounce
      back to their normal shape when you're through. Of course,
      if your normal shape is flat and perpendicular to your body,
      that's another story...

66. Don't worry if your hair is thinning. Use it as an excuse to start worrying funky hats: berets, bonnets, brown derbies, beanies with little propellers...

67. The next time a 20-something salesclerk looks you over and says, "We have swimsuits that can hide, like, any flaw," ask her "Where are the ones that can hide the fact that you're an idiot?"

68.   While dating a younger man is always a good idea, trolling the hallways at the local high school is not. Unless you have a hall pass.

69. Remember this: most of the things you can't remember anymore weren't worth remembering anyway. Remember this: most of the things you can't remember anymore weren't worth remembering anyway.

70. There are some benefits to fading eyesight. Now when your partner wants to show you the mistake you made in the checkbook, s/he has to stand in the other room to do it.

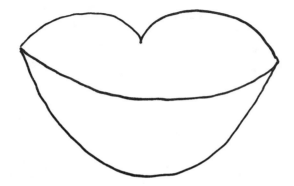

71.   If you decide to get that procedure done in which a doctor injects fat from your thighs into your lips, ask yourself this first: "If I go through with this, will I always wonder if my pants make my lips look fat?"

72.   Don't lie about your age – calculate it in dog years. After all, you never see a dog wondering whether to have her butt lifted for her next birthday.

73.   Did you know that 20% of women say their sex life is better after menopause? Of course, that could be due to memory loss. It's not that they forget how good sex was when they were young, it's that they forget where they live and end up having sex with their neighbor.

74.   A lot of midlife women have overactive bladders, which can make life a lot more interesting. For example, let's say you're at the dentist and she's halfway through cleaning your teeth when you have to pee. Just lean towards her, smile, and ask her hand you that little vacuum suction thingy. That ought to spice things up a bit.

75.   It may be time to visit Victoria's Secret or a sex therapist if you and your lover no longer sleep like spoons, you sleep like spatulas.

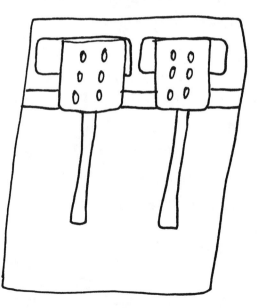

76. If someone gives you one of those joke packages for your birthday, with laxatives and denture cleaner and Depends, tell her mother. If you are her mother, ground her until she's middle aged, then give the "gift" back.

77. Another idea for a tattoo – two nipples right where yours used to be.

78.   If you look like a Ruebens painting, why not put a gold frame around your mirror and declare your reflection, "Art?" If you look like a Calvin Klein model, why not have a sandwich? And dessert?

79.   If you still insist on a bikini wax, get yours done at the car wash! Can't you just hear the guys there? "You won't believe what happened today! This broad went through the wax cycle on the roof of her car with her ass in the air!"

80.   Tried all the exercise videos and can't find one that works for you? Betcha haven't tried Body Heat! Okay, so it's not an exercise video. But it will get your pulse racing!

81.   Even if you had it all, some of it would get lost at the bottom of your purse and you'd never find it.

82.   Not every woman has night sweats as she goes through perimenopause and menopause. Many of us get night sweets - the irresistible urge to take Ben & Jerry to bed with us.

83.   You've already run with the wolves. You've run away from the wolves. Heck, you've even cleaned up after the wolves. Why not just sit back and howl at the moon for a while?

84.   If your sex drive is in low gear, maybe you should ask your doctor about Viagra. Just be forewarned, there are some nasty side effects, like thinking with your vulva.

85.   When you were a little girl, did you dress up as a fairy princess for Halloween every year? Or maybe as Batman? Well, who says you're too old for that now? Go ahead, wear a tiara or a full-body rubber suit, mask and cape to the grocery store. Maybe they'll even let your through the express line with more than ten items in your cart!

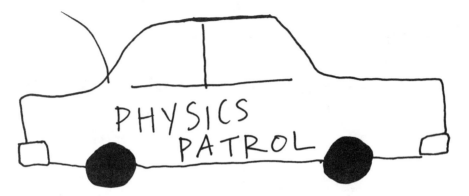

86.   Remember, it's the LAW of gravity, not the GUIDELINES of gravity. And even though that twenty-something at your office disobeyed the law today, it won't be long before she's pulled over by the gravity police.

87. If your husband takes up with a younger woman, find yourself a younger woman too. If that's not your thing, at least get a younger woman to clean your house. Believe me, you'll feel much better.

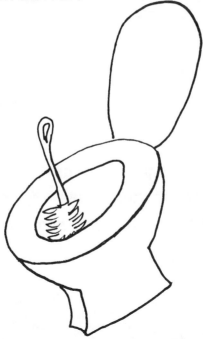

88.   Looking for a new exercise program? Try the Memory Loss
       Workout. Go to the kitchen. Now, try to remember why
       you're there. Walk back to the living room. Try to find your
       keys. Okay, breathe...

89.   Don't feel bad if you've tried all the positions in the Kama
        Sutra and failed.   Translated, "Kama Sutra" means "Ways to
        throw your back out."

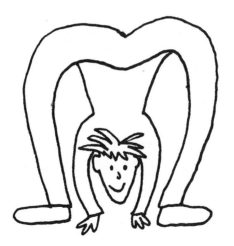

90.   Some of the things doctors do to stave off the aging process are too bizarre. Like injecting a toxic chemical into your face to paralyze your muscles. What's next? Injecting Jell-O into your breasts to make them firm and bouncy? This is one case where there's NOT always room for Jell-O!

91.   Just because your face is pressed up against the glass ceiling doesn't mean you're responsible for cleaning the smudge marks.

92.   Gingko is great for helping with memory problems. The only problem is, you have to remember to take it.

93. If you're fed up with your doctor, try Jiffy Lube & Pap. They promise to have you in and out of there in seconds. And they always top off your fluids for free.

94.　If you decide to use one of those new-fangled Kegel weights, make sure to get someone to spot you. Ask your personal trainer. After all, this is as personal as it gets.

95.　Have you ever wondered if turkeys think to themselves "Where did I get this people neck?"

96.   Remember, love means never having to say "You scum-sucking, bottom-dwelling, knuckle-dragging Neanderthal" more than once a day.

97.   Winter tip for hot-flashing women: Avoid making snow angels unless you're wearing a wet-suit.

98. Why do doctors always ask, "What day are you in your cycle?" Most of us can't remember our own names, how are we supposed to remember where we are in our cycles? What we need is an alarm clock that wakes us up with "Good morning, it's 72 degrees outside and Day 12 of your cycle. Have a nice day and don't forget to ovulate, if you can."

99. Varicose veins can come in handy; you can map out your next cross-country road trip on your legs.

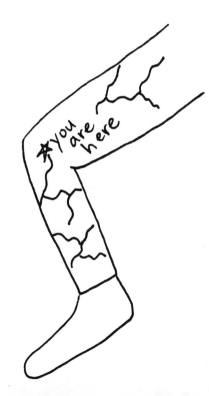

100. Memory tip: When lying about your age, you are supposed to subtract or divide years, not add or multiply. You may want to carry this handy little chart in your wallet:

Actual Age	Believable lie
38-50	26-32
51-60	33-47
61-70	48
70+	"Would you like to see my tiara and my Pulitzer prize?"

101. When your friends ask how you keep your skin looking so young, tell them you do acid. You don't have to tell them it's alpha hydroxy acid.

Glossary

Alpha Hydroxy Acid – The most abused drug among women 40-65. See your Yellow Pages for the 12-step program nearest you.

Bikini wax – Often used in lieu of an insanity plea in manslaughter trials.

Body Shaper – The newest female member of the World Wrestling Federation.

Botox – Yet another baseball player with a police record and an attitude problem.

Cellulite - A cell with an IQ lower than its circumference.

Co-enzyme Q - The answer you missed on the final in sophomore chemistry class.

Crone - A crane who was led astray and wound up on the wrong side of the law.

Crow's feet - Fine lines that appear on your face when you squint to read the tiny print on a bottle of anti-aging cream.

Denial - The ability to stare the facts in the face and refute them. A prerequisite for running for political office.

Duct tape – Cheaper than a WonderBra and often more effective.

Elasticity – As your body loses this, you tend to look for clothing that has more of it.

Estrogen – That kind of dumb girl you refused to befriend in junior high school and now you wish you had because she made a killing in Internet stocks.

Fountain of youth – (1) A leak in your kids' Slip & Slide; (2) when your kid pees in the public pool.

G-spot – Where gravity is strongest; usually anywhere you happen to be.

Gingko Biloba – A heavy metal band that always forgets lyrics halfway through the show.

Hormone replacement – What you may justifiably offer to do to any guy who calls you ma'am.

Hot flash – When you're sitting in a meeting and right in the middle of a boring presentation it occurs to you that you really don't have to wear pantyhose, no one can make you, and you'd like to see them try.

Kegel exercises – A great thing to do in line at the grocery store. For an extra bonus, count out loud and humiliate your kids.

Liposuction – What they really did during Alien Autopsy.

Love handles – What your spouse grabs you by as you go 'round and 'round on the airport carousel.

Mammogram – A telegram delivered by Pamela Lee Anderson (before her implants were removed).

May/December relationship – Any Hollywood movie pairing, e.g., Michele Pfeiffer/Robert Redford, Catherine Zeta-Jones/Sean Connery, Anne Heche/Harrison Ford, Me/Harrison Ford.

Memory loss – What?

Middle age – The period from the twelfth century to the fifteenth century when women with large white thighs were lusted after.

Mid-life – About the time you can expect parole.

Overactive bladder – A bladder who does too well on tests and raises the curve for the spleen, pancreas, and uvula. Often teased and called names like "Teacher's organ."

Perimenopause – The time between PMS and Menopause, otherwise known as "Give me a break!"

Personal growth – Those stray hairs on your chin; what your spouse/partner experiences when he/she points them out.

Plastic surgery – Removing all the Barbies from a room before entering.

Presbyopia – The inability to see Presbyterians close up.

Sex and Soy – Three letter words that are both good for you, but can be messy if spilled on the rug.

Tummy tuck – What happens when you try to get your shirt into your pants in a hurry. A lot better than a breast tuck.

Viagra – Miracle Grow for penises. Just be careful you don't get a green thumb applying it to your partner.

Victoria's Secret – She prefers teddy bears to teddies. They're soft and cuddly and don't ride up at awkward moments.

Wattle – The way you walk when you're back is out.

Yams – The only natural source of progesterone that you can serve at Thanksgiving.

About the Author

Leigh Anne Jasheway is not middle-aged, uh-uh, no way. She has naturally red hair (it occurs somewhere in nature). She is proud to say she can still wear her favorite college mini-skirt, although these days she wears it as a sweatband.

Leigh Anne graduated hubba-hubba cum laude from college, fully expecting to become Secretary of the Interior. Then someone told her she wouldn't get to wallpaper the redwoods, so she changed career paths, opting to hide out in graduate school until the student loan people caught up with her. Then, armed with a masters degree and Pontiac Ventura, she did a Thelma and Louise – playing both parts herself – driving, not over the edge of a cliff, but over a curb.

Today, she is married to a much younger man she picked up in a smoky bar where he couldn't see her crow's feet and she couldn't see the note his mom had pinned to his shirt with his address and phone number. They have two canine-American children (one is adopted) and grow organic mildew in Eugene, Oregon.

When not trying to find things she has misplaced, Leigh Anne runs a stand-up comedy troupe at a really slow pace. Last year, they came in last in the Boston Marathon, but considering they had to visit every port-a-can, it was quite an accomplishment.

About the Illustrator

When asked to illustrate this book, Deborah Kaye agreed, asking only one thing: that we tell the world that she is only 23, so there!